BOOKS BY ANTHONY HECHT

POETRY

*Flight Among the Tombs*  1998
*The Transparent Man*  1990
*Collected Earlier Poems*  1990
*The Venetian Vespers*  1979
*Millions of Strange Shadows*  1977
*The Hard Hours*  1967
*A Summoning of Stones*  1954

TRANSLATION

*Aeschylus's Seven Against Thebes*  1973
(with Helen Bacon)

ESSAYS AND CRITICISM

*On the Laws of the Poetic Art*  1995
(Andrew W. Mellon Lectures in the Fine Arts)
*The Hidden Law: The Poetry of W. H. Auden*  1993
*Obbligati*  1986

EDITOR

*The Essential George Herbert*  1987
*Jiggery-Pokery: A Compendium of Double Dactyls*  1967
(with John Hollander)

The Darkness and the Light

# The Darkness and the Light

*poems*

ANTHONY HECHT

Alfred A. Knopf   *New York*   2002

I am deeply grateful to Dorothea Tanning for her munificence, as well as her invincibly high spirits; to the Bogliasco Foundation and their Centro Studi Ligure, where a good number of these poems were written; to the Atlantic Center for the Arts, for their hospitality; to the Poetry Society of America, for the award of the Robert Frost Medal; and to the following journals in which recent poems have appeared: *The Forward, The Hudson Review, The New Republic, The New Yorker, The New York Review of Books, The Oxford Quarterly Review, The Paris Review, Pivot, Princeton University Library Chronicle, Rattapallax, The Sewanee Review, Sewanee Theological Review, The Southwest Review, Stand* (UK) and *The Yale Review.*

Grateful acknowledgment is made to Alfred A. Knopf and Faber and Faber Limited for permission to reprint an excerpt from "The Sun This March" from *Collected Poems* by Wallace Stevens, copyright © 1954 by Wallace Stevens. Rights in the United Kingdom administered by Faber and Faber Limited, London. Reprinted by permission of Alfred A. Knopf, a division of Random House, Inc., and Faber and Faber Limited.

Library of Congress Cataloging-in-Publication Data
Hecht, Anthony, [date]
The darkness and the light : poems / by Anthony Hecht.
p.  cm.
ISBN 0-375-70946-0 (tpb)
I. Title.
PS3558.E28 D37 2001
811'.54—dc21            00-062007

Manufactured in the United States of America
Published June 20, 2001
First paperback edition, June 2002

*For Helen*

*and*

*In Memory of Harry and Kathleen Ford*

*and of William and Emily Maxwell*

*Aye, on the shores of darkness there is light.*

—John Keats


*The exceeding brightness of this early sun*
*Makes me conceive how dark I have become,*

. . . . . . . . . . . . . .

*Oh! Rabbi, rabbi, fend my soul for me*
*And a true savant of this dark nature be.*

—Wallace Stevens

# Contents

Late Afternoon: The Onslaught of Love     3

Circles     5

Memory     7

Mirror     8

Samson     10

An Orphic Calling     11

Rara Avis in Terris     13

A Fall     15

Haman     17

A Certain Slant     18

A Brief Account of Our City     19

Saul and David     22

Despair     24

The Hanging Gardens of Tyburn     25

Judith     26

Illumination     27

Look Deep     28

Nocturne: A Recurring Dream     30

Lot's Wife     31

Public Gardens     32

Sacrifice     33

The Witch of Endor     39

Indolence    40

The Ashen Light of Dawn (Baudelaire)    41

The Plastic and the Poetic Form (Goethe)    43

The Bequest (Vaillant)    44

Once More, with Feeling
    (Charles d'Orléans)    45

Le Jet d'Eau (Baudelaire)    46

Taking Charge (Charles d'Orléans)    48

A Symposium (Horace)    49

A Special Occasion (Horace)    50

A Prayer to Twin Divinities (Horace)    51

Miriam    52

Witness    53

Lapidary Inscription with Explanatory
    Note    54

Long-Distance Vision    55

Secrets    57

Poppy    58

The Ceremony of Innocence    59

The Road to Damascus    60

Elders    61

Sarabande on Attaining the Age of
    Seventy-seven    63

I.M.E.M.    64

"The Darkness and the Light
    Are Both Alike to Thee"    65

Notes    66

# The Darkness and the Light

# Late Afternoon: The Onslaught of Love

At this time of day
One could hear the caulking irons sound
Against the hulls in the dockyard.
Tar smoke rose between trees
And large oily patches floated on the water,
Undulating unevenly
In the purple sunlight
Like the surfaces of Florentine bronze.

At this time of day
Sounds carried clearly
Through hot silences of fading daylight.
The weedy fields lay drowned
In odors of creosote and salt.
Richer than double-colored taffeta,
Oil floated in the harbor,
Amoeboid, iridescent, limp.
It called to mind the slender limbs
Of Donatello's *David*.

It was lovely and she was in love.
They had taken a covered boat to one of the islands.
The city sounds were faint in the distance:
Rattling of carriages, tumult of voices,
Yelping of dogs on the decks of barges.

At this time of day
Sunlight empurpled the world.
The poplars darkened in ranks
Like imperial servants.
Water lapped and lisped
In its native and quiet tongue.
Oakum was in the air and the scent of grasses.
There would be fried smelts and cherries and cream.
Nothing designed by Italian artisans
Would match this evening's perfection.
The puddled oil was a miracle of colors.

# Circles

Long inventories of miseries unspoken,
Appointment books of pain,
Attars of love gone rancid, the pitcher broken
At the fountain, rooted unkindnesses:
All were implied by her, by me suspected,
At her saying, "I could not bear
Ever returning to that village in Maine.
For me the very air,
The harbor smells, the hills, all are infected."

I gave my sympathy, filled in the blanks
With lazy, bitter fictions,
And, feeling nothing, won her grateful thanks.

Many long years and some attachments later
I was to be instructed by the courts
Upon the nicest points of such afflictions,
Having become a weakened, weekend father.
All of us, in our own circle of hell
(Not that of forger, simonist or pander),
Patrolled the Olmsted bosks of Central Park,
Its children-thronged resorts,
Pain-tainted ground,
Where the innocent and the fallen join to play
In the fields, if not of the Lord, then of the Law;
Which decreed that love be hobbled and confined
To Saturday,
Trailing off into Sunday-before-dark;

And certain sandpits, slides, swings, monkey bars
Became the old thumbscrews of spoiled affection
And agonized aversion.
Of these, the most tormenting
In its single-songed, maddening monotony,
Its glaring-eyed and nostril-flaring steeds
With perfect teeth, but destined never to win
Their countless and interminable races,
Was the merry, garish, mirthless carousel.

# Memory

Sepia oval portraits of the family,
Black-framed, adorned the small brown-papered hall,
But the parlor was kept unused, never disturbed.
Under a glass bell, the dried hydrangeas
Had bleached to the hue of ancient newspaper,
Though once, someone affirmed, they had been pink.
Pink still were the shiny curling orifices
Of matching seashells stationed on the mantel
With mated, spiked, wrought-iron candlesticks.
The room contained a tufted ottoman,
A large elephant-foot umbrella stand
With two malacca canes, and two peacock
Tail-feathers sprouting from a small-necked vase.
On a teak side table lay, side by side,
A Bible and a magnifying glass.
Green velvet drapes kept the room dark and airless
Until on sunny days toward midsummer
The brass andirons caught a shaft of light
For twenty minutes in late afternoon
In a radiance dimly akin to happiness—
The dusty gleam of temporary wealth.

# Mirror

*for J. D. McClatchy*

Always halfway between you and your double,
Like Washington, I cannot tell a lie.
When the dark queen demands in her querulous treble,
"Who is the fairest?," inaudibly I reply,

"Beauty, your highness, dwells in the clouded cornea
Of the self-deceived beholder, whereas Truth,
According to film moguls of California,
Lies in makeup, smoke and mirrors, gin and vermouth,

Or the vinous second-pressings of *Veritas*,
Much swilled at Harvard. The astronomer's speculum
Reveals it, and to the politician's cheval glass
It's that part of a horse he cannot distinguish from

His elbow; but it's also the upside-down
Melodies of Bach fugues, the right-to-left
Writing of Leonardo, a long-term loan
From Hebrew, retrograde fluencies in deft,

Articulate penmanship. An occasional Louis
Might encounter it in the corridors of Versailles;
It evades the geometrician's confident QE
D, but the constant motion from ground to sky

And back again of the terrible Ferris wheel
Sackville describes in *A Mirror for Magistrates*
Conveys some semblance of the frightening feel
Of the mechanical heartlessness of Fate,

The ring-a-ding-*Ding-an-Sich*. Yet think how gaily
In the warped fun-house glass our flesh dissolves
In shape and helpless laughter, unlike the Daily
Mirror in which New Yorkers saw themselves.

It's when no one's around that I'm most truthful,
In a world as timeless as before The Fall.
No one to reassure that she's still youthful,
I gaze untroubled at the opposite wall.

Light fades, of course, with the oncoming of dusk;
I faithfully note the rheostat dial of day
That will rise to brilliance, weaken as it must
Through each uncalibrated shade of gray,

One of them that of winter afternoons,
Desolate, leaden, and in its burden far
Deeper than darkness, engrossing in its tones
Those shrouded regions where the meanings are."

# Samson

There came to the nameless wife of Manoah
In annunciation an angel who declared:
"Like Sarah who was barren, even so shall you
Conceive a child; you also shall bear a son."

> Almost every day at the Boston Lying-In
> There are births defying expectation, all
> Medical wisdom; almost daily a mother thinks
> Her child God-given, a miracle and a wonder.

And the angel said: "You must both abstain from wine,
You and the child; from all contact with the dead;
Nor let your hair be shorn, for he is God's,
And he shall be a Nazarite from the womb."

> In the Hebrew shul at Lodz the little boys
> Studied the Torah, and let their sidelocks curl
> And sway to the rhythm of reading. They too have
>     been
> Sacrificed, like Nazarites before them.

# An Orphic Calling

*for Mihaly Csikszentmihalyi*


The stream's *courante* runs on, a *force majeure*,
A Major rippling of the pure mind of Bach,
Tumult of muscled currents, formed in far
Reaches of edelweiss, cloud and alpenstock,

Now folding into each other, flexing, swirled
In cables of perdurable muscle-tones,
Hurrying through this densely noted world,
Small chambers, studio mikes, Concorde headphones,

And from deep turbulent rapids, roiled and spun,
They rise in watery cycles to those proud
And purifying heights where they'd begun
On Jungfrau cliffs of edelweiss and cloud,

Piled cumuli, that *fons et origo*
("Too lofty and original to rage")
Of the mind's limpid unimpeded flow
Where freedom and necessity converge

And meet in a fresh curriculum of love
(Minor in grief, major in happiness)
As interlocking melodies contrive
Small trysts and liaisons, briefly digress

But only to return to Interlaken
Altitudes of clear trebles, crystal basses,
Fine reconciliations and unbroken
Threadings of fern-edged flutes down tumbling races.

An Orphic calling it is, one that invites
Responsories, a summons to lute-led
Nature, as morning's cinnabar east ignites
And the instinctive sunflower turns its head.

# Rara Avis in Terris

*for Helen*

Hawks are in the ascendant. Just look about.
  Cormorants, ravens, jailbirds of ominous wing
Befoul the peace, their caws
                    raised in some summoning
    To an eviscerating cause,
      Some jihad, some rash all-get-out
  Crusade, leaving the field all gore and guano
  Justified in hysterical soprano

By balding buzzards who brandish the smart bomb,
  The fractured atom in their unclipped talons.
Ruffling with all the pride
                  of testosteronic felons,
    They storm the airwaves with implied
    Threats and theatrical aplomb
  Or cruise the sky with delta stealth and gelid
  Chestsful of combat-decorative fruit salad.

It's the same in the shady groves of academe:
  Cold eye and primitive beak and callused foot
Conjunctive to destroy
               all things of high repute,
    Whole epics, Campion's songs, Tolstoy,
    Euclid and logic's enthymeme,
  As each man bares his scalpel, whets his saber,
  As though enjoined to deconstruct his neighbor.

And that's not the worst of it; there are the Bacchae,
	The ladies' auxiliary of the raptor clan
With their bright cutlery,
					sororal to a man.
		And feeling peckish, they foresee
		An avian banquet in the sky,
	Feasting off dead white European males,
	Or local living ones, if all else fails.


But where are the mild monogamous lovebirds,
	Parakeets, homing pigeons, sundry doves,
Beringed, bewitching signs
					of the first, greatest loves
		Eros or Agape gently defines?
		God's for the ark's small flocks and herds,
	Or Venus incarnate as that quasi-queen
	Of France known as Diane de la Poitrine.


They are here, my dear, they are here in the marble air,
	According to the micro-Mosaic law,
Miraculously aloft
					above that flood and flaw
		Where Noah darkly plies his craft.
		Lightly an olive branch they bear,
	Its deathless leafage emblematic of
	A quarter-century of faultless love.

# A Fall

Those desolate, brute, chilling sublimities,
Unchanging but as the light may chance to fall,
Deserts of snow, forlorn barrens of rock,
What could be more indifferent to man's life
Than your average Alp, stripped to the blackened bone
Above the tree line, except where the ice rags,
Patches, and sheets of winter cling yearlong?
The cowbell's ludicrous music, the austere
Sobrieties of Calvin, precision watches,
A cheese or two, and that is all the Swiss
Have given the world, unless we were to cite
The questionable morals of their banks.
But how are people to live in dignity
When at two p.m. the first shadows of night,
Formed by the massive shoulder of some slope,
Cast, for the rest of the day, entire valleys—
Their window boxes of geraniums,
Their cobbles, pinecones, banners and coffee cups—
Into increasing sinks and pools of dark?
And that is but half the story. The opposing slope
Keeps morning from its flaxen charities
Until, on midsummer days, eleven-thirty,
When fresh birdsong and cow dung rinse the air
And all outdoors still glistens with night-dew.
All this serves to promote a state of mind
Cheerless and without prospects. But yesterday
I let myself, in spite of dark misgivings,

Be talked into a strenuous excursion
Along one high ridge promising a view.
And suddenly, at a narrowing of the path,
The whole earth fell away, and dizzily
I beheld the most majestic torrent in Europe,
A pure cascade, over six hundred feet,
Falling straight down—it was like Rapunzel's hair,
But white, as if old age and disappointment
Had left her bereft of suitors. Down it plunged,
Its great, continuous, unending weight
Toppling from above in a long shaft
Or carven stem that broke up at its base
Into enormous rhododendron blooms
Of spray, a dense array of shaken blossoms.
I teetered perilously, scared and dazed,
And slowly, careful of both hand and foot,
Made my painstaking way back down the trail.
That evening in my bedroom I recalled
The scene's terror and grandeur, my vertigo
Mixed with a feeling little short of awe.
And I retraced my steps in the secure
Comfort of lamplight on a Baedeker.
That towering waterfall I just had viewed
At what had seemed the peril of my life
Was regarded locally with humorous
Contempt, and designated the *Pisse-Vache*.

# Haman

I am Haman the Hangman, the engineer
And chief designer of that noble structure,
The Gallows. Let the Jews tremble and beware:
I have made preparations for their capture
And extirpation in a holy war
Against their foolish faith, their hateful culture,
An ethnic cleansing that will leave us pure,
Ridding the world of this revolting creature.
I shall have camps, *Arbeit Macht Frei*, the lure
Of hope, the chastening penalty of torture,
And other entertainments of despair,
The which I hanker after like a lecher.
And best of all the gibbet, my friend, my poor
One-armed assistant, in stiff, obedient posture,
Like a young officer's salute, but more
Rigid, and more instructive than a lecture,
Saying, "I can teach you to tread on air,
And add another cubit to your stature."

# A Certain Slant

Etched on the window were barbarous thistles of frost,
Edged everywhere in that tame winter sunlight
With pavé diamonds and fine prickles of ice
Through which a shaft of the late afternoon
Entered our room to entertain the sway
And float of motes, like tiny aqueous lives,
Then glanced off the silver teapot, raising stains
Of snailing gold upcast across the ceiling,
And bathed itself at last in the slop bucket
Where other aqueous lives, equally slow,
Turned in their sad, involuntary courses,
Swiveled in eel-green broth. Who could have known
Of any elsewhere? Even of out-of-doors,
Where the stacked firewood gleamed in drapes of glaze
And blinded the sun itself with jubilant theft,
The smooth cool plunder of celestial fire?

# A Brief Account of Our City

*for Dorothea Tanning*

If you approach our city from the south,
The first thing that you'll see is the Old Fort,
High on its rock. Its crenellated walls,
Dungeons and barbicans and towers date back
To the eighth century. The local barons
Of hereditary title moved their courts
Inside whenever they were under siege
With all their retinues, taxing the poor,
Feuding with neighboring baronies, masterful
Only in greed and management of arms.
Great murderous vulgar men, they must have been.
The fort, history records, was never taken.
It might be worth a visit when you come.
For a mere thirty kroner you can ascend
The turrets for a quite incomparable view.
From there our forests look a lot like parsley
And cress; there the wind enters your throat
Like an iced mountain stream. Piled here and there
You will find pyramids of cannonballs
In the great courtyard, stacked like croquembouches,
Warm to the touch where the sun glances off them
And chilly in the shade. The arsenal,
Containing arquebuses, fruitwood bows,
As well as heavy mortars and great cannons,

Is open to the public. The furniture
Is solid, thick and serviceable stuff,
No nonsense. But what may strike you most of all
Is the plain, barren spareness of the rooms.
No art here. Nothing to appease the eye.
And not because such things have been removed
To our museums. This was the way they lived:
In self-denying, plain austerity.
As you draw nearer to the city itself
You will make out, beyond the citadel,
The shapely belfry of Our Lady of Sorrows.
Then you will see, in the midst of a great field,
Surrounded on all sides by acres of wheat,
A large, well-cared-for, isolated house—
No others neighboring, or even within view—
Which is given free of charge by the city board
To the Public Executioner. His children
Are allowed a special tutor, but not admitted
To any of our schools. The family
Can raise all that's required for their meals
Right on the grounds, and, if need be, a doctor
Will call on them, given half a day's notice.
The children are forbidden to leave the place,
As is, indeed, the entire family,
Except when the father alone is called upon
To perform official duties. And by this means
Everyone is kept happy; our citizens
Need have no fear of encountering any of them,

While they live comfortably at our expense.
Whenever you visit, be certain that you dine
At one of our fine restaurants; don't miss
The Goldene Nockerl, which for potato dumplings
Cannot be matched, and our rich amber beer
Is widely known as the finest in this region.

# Saul and David

It was a villainous spirit, snub-nosed, foul
Of breath, thick-taloned and malevolent,
That squatted within him wheresoever he went
      And possessed the soul of Saul.

There was no peace on pillow or on throne.
In dreams the toothless, dwarfed, and squinny-eyed
Started a joyful rumor that he had died
      Unfriended and alone.

The doctors were confounded. In his distress, he
Put aside arrogant ways and condescended
To seek among the flocks where they were tended
      By the youngest son of Jesse,

A shepherd boy, but goodly to look upon,
Unnoticed but God-favored, sturdy of limb
As Michelangelo later imagined him,
      Comely even in his frown.

Shall a mere shepherd provide the cure of kings?
Heaven itself delights in ironies such
As this, in which a boy's fingers would touch
      Pythagorean strings

And by a modal artistry assemble
The very Sons of Morning, the ranked and choired
Heavens in sweet laudation of the Lord,
    And make Saul cease to tremble.

# Despair

Sadness. The moist gray shawls of drifting sea-fog,
Salting scrub pine, drenching the cranberry bogs,
Erasing all but foreground, making a ghost
Of anyone who walks softly away;
And the faint, penitent psalmody of the ocean.

Gloom. It appears among the winter mountains
On rainy days. Or the tiled walls of the subway
In caged and aging light, in the steel scream
And echoing vault of the departing train,
The vacant platform, the yellow destitute silence.

But despair is another matter. Midafternoon
Washes the worn bank of a dry arroyo,
Its ocher crevices, unrelieved rusts,
Where a startled lizard pauses, nervous, exposed
To the full glare of relentless marigold sunshine.

# The Hanging Gardens of Tyburn

Mysteriously fed by the dying breath
Of felons, by the foul odor that melts
Down from their bodies hanging on the gallows,
The rank, limp flesh, the soft pendulous guilts,

This solitary plant takes root at night,
Its tiny charnel blossoms the pale blue
Of Pluto's ice pavilions; being dried,
Powdered and mixed with the cold morning dew

From the left hand of an executed man,
It confers untroubled sleep, and can prevent
Prenatal malformations if applied
To a woman's swelling body, except in Lent.

Take care to clip only the little blossoms,
For the plant, uprooted, utters a cry of pain
So highly pitched as both to break the eardrum
And render the would-be harvester insane.

# Judith

It took less valor than I'm reputed for.
Since I was a small child I have hated men.
Even the feeblest, in their fantasies,
Triumph as sexual athletes, putting the shot
Squarely between the thighs of some meek woman,
While others strut like decathlon champions,
Like royal David hankering after his neighbor's
Dutiful wife. For myself, I found a husband
Not very prepossessing, but very rich.
Neither of us was interested in children.
In my case, the roving hands, the hot tumescence of an uncle,
Weakened my taste for close intimacies.
Ironically, heaven had granted me
What others took to be attractive features
And an alluring body, and which for years
Instinctively I looked upon with shame.
All men seemed stupid in their lecherous,
Self-flattering appetites, which I found repugnant.
But at last, as fate would have it, I found a chance
To put my curse to practical advantage.
It was easy. Holofernes was pretty tight;
I had only to show some cleavage and he was done for.

# Illumination

Ground lapis for the sky, and scrolls of gold,
Before which shepherds kneel, gazing aloft
At visiting angels clothed in egg-yolk gowns,
Celestial tinctures smuggled from the East,
From sunlit Eden, the palmed and plotted banks
Of sun-tanned Aden. Brought home in fragile grails,
Planted in England, rising at Eastertide,
Their petals cup stamens of topaz dust,
The powdery stuff of cooks and cosmeticians.
But to the camel's-hair tip of the finest brush
Of Brother Anselm, it is the light of dawn,
Gilding the hems, the sleeves, the fluted pleats
Of the antiphonal archangelic choirs
Singing their melismatic *pax in terram.*
The child lies cribbed below, in bestial dark,
Pale as the tiny tips of crocuses
That will find their way to the light through drifts of snow.

# Look Deep

Look deep into my eyes. Think to yourself,
"There is 'the fringèd curtain' where a play
Will shortly be enacted." Look deep down
Into the pupil. Think, "I am going to sleep."

The pupil has its many-tinctured curtain
Of moiré silks, parted to let you in,
And the play will present a goddess you used to know
From the glint of sunlit fountain, from beveled mirror,

A goddess, yes, but only a messenger
Whose message is the armorial fleur-de-lys
She carries in her right hand, signifying
The majesty of France, as handed down

From the royal house of Solomon and David:
Wisdom, music and valor gracefully joined
In trefoil heraldry. Nearly asleep,
You settle down for a full-scale production

Of *The Rainstorm* in its grand entirety,
Which, greater than *The Ring*, lasts forty nights;
Everything huddled in one rocking stateroom,
A saving remnant, a life-raft-world in little.

Dream at your ease of the dark forests of spruce
Swaying in currents of green, gelatinous winds

Above which the classless zoo and zookeepers
Weather the testing and baptismal waters;

Dream of the long, undeviating gloom,
The unrelenting skies, the pounding wet
Through which a peak will thrust, a light, and over
The covenanted ark, an *arc-en-ciel.*

# Nocturne: A Recurring Dream

The moon is a pearl in mist and sets the scene.
Comfort seems within reach, just over there,
But rocks, water, and darkness intervene.

Incalculable dangers lie between
Us and the warmth of bedding, the fire's flare.
The moon is a pearl in mist and sets the scene;

She's not, as claimed Ben Jonson, heaven's queen.
More ghostly, an omen of death hung in the air.
Rocks, water, and darkness intervene

Between that shadowy dwelling, barely seen,
And something not at all unlike despair.
The moon is a pearl in mist and sets the scene

For—secret rites? Ensorcellment? Marine
Catastrophe? Before we can declare,
Rocks, water, and darkness intervene.

Oystery pale, anything but serene,
Our goal seems cloaked in the forbidding glare
Of moonlight as a pearl that sets the scene
Where rocks, water, and darkness intervene.

# Lot's Wife

How simple the pleasures of those childhood days,
Simple but filled with exquisite satisfactions.
The iridescent labyrinth of the spider,
Its tethered tensor nest of polygons
Puffed by the breeze to a little bellying sail—
Merely observing this gave infinite pleasure.
The sound of rain. The gentle graphite veil
Of rain that makes of the world a steel engraving,
Full of soft fadings and faint distances.
The self-congratulations of a fly,
Rubbing its hands. The brown bicameral brain
Of a walnut. The smell of wax. The feel
Of sugar to the tongue: a delicious sand.
One understands immediately how Proust
Might cherish all such postage-stamp details.
Who can resist the charms of retrospection?

# Public Gardens

"Flow'rs of all hue," a sightless Milton wrote
Of Paradise, which doesn't mean "all flowers."
An impoverished exile in his loneliest hours
Knows that not everybody makes the boat.

He has not mastered the language, he still retains
A craving for some remembered native dishes;
These sorrowful foreign skies, all smoke and ashes,
Remain uncleansed by the pummeling winter rains.

Jobless, he mopes in the shabby public gardens
Where importunate pigeons harry him for food.
Back in the dark unwelcome solitude
Of his attic room, he can view through the daisied curtains

The pantile roofs of this dirty little port.
But without passport or valid papers his fate
Lies with officials. Immense reasons of state
Conjoin to deny him permission to depart.

His is a sad but not uncommon lot,
Familiar to border guards, to police and such.
Even plantain, spleenwort, lichen, tuber and vetch
May be found in Paradise; the teasel not.

# Sacrifice

Long years, and I found favor
In the sight of the Lord, who brought me out of Ur
        To where his promise lay,
        There with him to confer
On Justice and Mercy and the appointed day
        Of Sodom's ashen fate;
For me he closeted sweetness in the date,
        And gave to salt its savor.

Three promises he gave,
Came like three kings or angels to my door:
        His purposes concealed
        In coiled and kerneled store
He planted as a seedling that would yield
        In my enfeebled years
A miracle that would command my tears
        With piercings of the grave.

"Old man, behold Creation,"
Said the Lord, "the leaping hills, the thousand-starred
        Heavens and watery floor.
        Is anything too hard
For the Lord, who shut all seas within their doors?"
        And then, for his name's sake
He led me, knowing where my heart would break,
        Into temptation.

The whole of my long life
Pivoted on one terrible day at dawn.
    Isaac, my son, and I
    Were to Moriah gone.
There followed an hour in which I wished to die,
    Being visited by these things:
My name called out, the beat of gigantic wings,
    Faggots, and flame, and knife.

## II
### ISAAC

Youthful I was and trusting and strong of limb,
The fresh-split firewood roped tight to my back,
And I bore unknowing that morning my funeral pyre.
My father, face averted, carried the flame,
And, in its scabbard, the ritual blade he bore.
It seemed to me at the time a wearisome trek.

I thought of my mother, how, in her age, the Lord
Had blessed her among women, giving her me
As joke and token both, unlikelihood
Being his way. But where, where from our herd
Was the sacrifice, I asked my father. He,
In a spasm of agony, bound me hand and foot.

I thought, *I am poured out like water, like wax*
*My heart is melted in the midst of my bowels.*
Both were tear-blinded. Hate and love and fear
Wrestled to ruin us, savage us beyond cure.
And the fine blade gleamed with the fury of live coals
Where we had reared an altar among the rocks.

Peace be to us both, to father Abraham,
To me, elected the shorn stunned lamb of God—
We were sentenced and reprieved by the same Voice—
And to all our seed, by this terror sanctified,
To be numbered even as the stars at the small price
Of an old scapegoated and thicket-baffled ram.

III

1945

It was widely known that the army of occupation
Was in full retreat. The small provincial roads
Rumbled now every night with tanks and trucks,
Echoed with cries in German, much *mach schnell,*
*Zurück, ganz richtig, augenblicklich, jawohl,*
Audible in the Normandy countryside.
So it had been for days, or, rather, nights,
The troops at first making their moves in darkness,
But pressures of haste toward the end of March
Left stragglers to make their single ways alone,
At their own risk, and even in daylight hours.

Since the soldiers were commandeering anything
They needed—food, drink, vehicles of all sorts—
One rural family dismantled their bicycle,
Daubed the chrome parts—rims, sprocket, spokes—with
    mud,
And wired them carefully to the upper boughs
Of the orchard. And the inevitable came
In the shape of a young soldier, weighted down
With pack and bedroll, rifle, entrenching tools,
Steel helmet and heavy boots just after dawn.
The family was at breakfast. He ordered them out
In front of the house with abusive German words
They couldn't understand, but gesture and rifle

Made his imperious wishes perfectly clear.
They stood in a huddled group, all nine of them.
And then he barked his furious command:
*Fahrrad!* They all looked blank. He shouted again:
*FAHRRAD! FAHRRAD! FAHRRAD!*, as though sheer
    volume
Joined with his anger would make his meaning plain.
The father of the family experimentally
Inquired, *Manger?* The soldier, furious,
At last dredged up an explosive *Bicyclette,*
Proud of himself, contemptuous of them.
To this the father in a small pantomime—
Shrugged shoulders, palms turned out, a helpless, long,
Slow shaking of the head, then the wide gesture
Of an arm, taking in all his property—
Conveyed *Nous n'avons pas de bicyclettes*
More clearly than his words. To the young soldier
This seemed unlikely. No one could live this far
From neighbors, on a poor untraveled road
That lacked phone lines, without the usual means
Of transport. There was no time to search
The house, the barn, cowsheds, coops, pens and grounds.
He looked at the frightened family huddled together,
And with the blunt nose of his rifle barrel
Judiciously singled out the eldest son,
A boy perhaps fourteen, but big for his years,
Obliging him to place himself alone
Against the whitewashed front wall of the house.
Then, at the infallible distance of ten feet,

With rifle pointed right at the boy's chest,
The soldier shouted what was certainly meant
To be his terminal order: *BICYCLETTE!*

It was still early on a chilly morning.
The water in the tire-treads of the road
Lay clouded, polished pale and chalked with frost,
Like the paraffin-sealed coverings of preserves.
The very grass was a stiff lead-crystal gray,
Though splendidly prismatic where the sun
Made its slow way between the lingering shadows
Of nearby fence posts and more distant trees.
There was leisure enough to take full note of this
In the most minute detail as the soldier held
Steady his index finger on the trigger.

It wasn't charity. Perhaps mere prudence,
Saving a valuable round of ammunition
For some more urgent crisis. Whatever it was,
The soldier reslung his rifle on his shoulder,
Turned wordlessly and walked on down the road
The departed German vehicles had taken.

There followed a long silence, a long silence.
For years they lived together in that house,
Through daily tasks, through all the family meals,
In agonized, unviolated silence.

# The Witch of Endor

I had the gift, and arrived at the technique
That called up spirits from the vasty deep
To traffic with our tumid flesh, to speak
Of the unknown regions where the buried keep
Their counsel, but for such talents I was banned
By Saul himself from sortilege and spell
Who banished thaumaturges from the land
Where in their ignorance the living dwell.

But then he needed me; he was sore afraid,
And begged for forbidden commerce with the dead.
Samuel he sought, and I raised up that shade,
Laggard, resentful, with shawl-enfolded head,
Who spoke a terrible otherworldly curse
In a hollow, deep, engastrimythic voice.

# Indolence

Beyond the corruption both of rust and moth,
I loaf and invite my soul, calmly I slump
On the crowded sidewalk, blissed to the gills on hemp;
Mine is a sanctified and holy sloth.

The guilty and polluted come to view
My meek tranquility, the small tin cup
That sometimes runneth over. They fill it up
To assuage the torments they are subject to,

And hasten to the restoratives of sin,
While I, a flower-child, beautiful and good,
Remain inert, as St. Matthew said I should:
I rest, I toil not, neither do I spin.

Think how this sound economy of right
And wrong wisely allows me to confer
On all the bustling who in their bustling err
Consciences of a pure and niveous white.

# The Ashen Light of Dawn

Reveille was bugled through army camps
As a soft dawn wind was fluttering streetlamps.

It was that hour when smooth sun-tanned limbs
Of adolescents twitched with unlawful dreams,
When, like a bloodshot eye beside the bed,
A nightlamp soaked oncoming day in red,
When, weighted beneath a humid body's brawn,
The soul mimicked that duel of lamp and dawn.
Like a face dried by the wind of recent tears,
The air is rife with whatever disappears,
And woman wearies of love, man of his chores.

Here and there chimneys smoked. The local whores,
Mascara'ed, overpainted, slept a stone
And stupid sleep, while the impoverished crone,
Breasts limp and frigid, alternately blew
On embers and on fingers, both going blue.
It was the hour of grief, of chill, of want;
Women in childbirth felt their seizures mount;
Like a thick, blood-choked scream, a rooster crowed
Distantly from some dim, befogged abode
As a sea of fog englutted the city blocks,
And in some seedy hospice, human wrecks
Breathed their death-rattling last, while debauchees
Tottered toward home, drained of their powers to please.

All pink and green in flounces, Aurora strolled
The vacant Seine embankments as the old,
Stupefied, blear-eyed Paris, glum and resigned,
Laid out his tools to begin the daily grind.

BAUDELAIRE

# The Plastic and the Poetic Form

Let that Greek youth out of clay
    Mold an urn to fashion
Beauty, gladdening the eye
    With deft-handed vision.

But the poet's sterner test
    Urges him to seize on
A Euphrates of unrest,
    Fluid in evasion.

Duly bathed and cooled, his mind,
    Ardorless, will utter
Liquid song, his forming hand
    Lend a shape to water.

GOETHE

# The Bequest

Good folk, my love's abandoned me.
Whoever gets her, willingly
(Although she's kind as well as fair)
I give her to him as my heir,
Blithe, easy, unencumbered, free.

She wields her graces cunningly,
And God knows her fidelity.
Let him who wins her next take care.
Good folk, my love's abandoned me.

Let him look after her and see
She's kept from smirch and calumny
Because the darling thing might snare
Any man's heart who's unaware.
Forlorn I make my threnody:
Good folk, my love's abandoned me.

VAILLANT

# Once More, with Feeling

The world has doffed her outerwear
Of chilling wind and teeming rain,
And donned embroidery again,
Tailored with sunlight's gilded flair.

No beast of field nor bird of air
But sings or bellows this refrain:
"The world has doffed her outerwear
Of chilling wind and teeming rain."

Fountain, millrace and river spare
No costly beading nor abstain
From silvered liveries of grosgrain.
All is new-clad and debonair.
The world has doffed her outerwear.

CHARLES D'ORLÉANS

# Le Jet d'Eau

My dear, your lids are weary;
Lower them, rest your eyes—
As though some languid pleasure
Wrought on you by surprise.
The tattling courtyard fountain
Repeats this night's excess
In fervent, ceaseless tremors
Of murmur and caress.

> A spray of petaled brilliance
>    That uprears
> In gladness as the Moon-
>    Goddess appears
> Falls like an opulent glistening
>    Of tears.

Even thus, your soul, exalted,
Primed by the body's joys,
Ascends in quenchless cravings
To vast, enchanted skies,
And then brims over, dying
In swoons, faint and inert,
And drains to the silent, waiting,
Dark basin of my heart.

A spray of petaled brilliance
    That uprears
In gladness as the Moon-
    Goddess appears
Falls like an opulent glistening
    Of tears.


You, whom the night makes radiant,
How amorous to lie, spent,
Against your breasts and listen
To the fountain's soft lament.
O Moon, melodious waters,
Wind-haunted trees in leaf,
Your melancholy mirrors
My ardors and their grief.

A spray of petaled brilliance
    That uprears
In gladness as the Moon-
    Goddess appears
Falls like an opulent glistening
    Of tears.

BAUDELAIRE

# Taking Charge

Back off, clear out, the lot of you,
Vile Melancholy, Spleen, and Woe;
Think you to dog me to and fro
As in the past you used to do?

Not anymore. "Begone. You're through,"
Says Reason, your determined foe.
Back off, clear out, the lot of you,
Vile Melancholy, Spleen, and Woe.

If you resurface, may God throw
You and your whole damnable crew
Back where you came from down below,
And thereby give the fiend his due.
Back off, clear out, the lot of you.

CHARLES D'ORLÉANS

# A Symposium

Only a Thracian goon would lurch from tippling
To brawling. Barbarians one and all. For our part
Let's preserve the rites of Bacchus, our seemly and civil
Devotions in the calm service of pleasure.
Good wine imbibed by lamplight has nothing to do
With bashed-in cups or swordplay. Subdue your clamor,
My friends, and use your well-connected elbows
For hoisting moderate drinks. You ask that I
Knock back my own full share of Falernian must.
Then let's hear Megylla's brother tell us who knocked him
All of a heap with the heavy weapons of bliss.
Suddenly tongue-tied? Well then, I'm swearing off,
Not a drop more. Those are my fixed conditions.
Whichever beauty it was that sent you reeling,
There's nothing to blush about, since you only go
For the classy and high-toned. Come on, just whisper
Her name in my ear.                    O you poor silly kid,
You've bought yourself a regular Charybdis;
You deserve better. What can Thessalian spells,
Wizards or magic ointments do for you now?
Snagged by the tripartite, hybrid beast, Chimera,
Not even Bellerophon, mounted on Pegasus, could save you.

HORACE I.xxvii

49

# A Special Occasion

O *mise-en-bouteille* in the very year of my birth
And Manlius' consulship, celestial spirits,
Instinct with ardors, slugfests, the sighs of lovers,
Hilarity and effortless sleep, whatever,
Campanian harvest, well-sealed special reserve
For some fine and festive holiday, descend
From your high cellarage, since my friend Corvinus,
A connoisseur, has called for a more mature wine.
Soaked though he be in vintage Socratic wisdom,
He's not going to snub you. For even Cato the Elder,
All Roman rectitude, would warm to a drink.

You limber the dullard's faculties with your proddings;
With Bacchus the Trickster you break through careful
    discretion,
Making even the politic say what they mean.
You resurrect hope in the most dejected of minds;
To the poor and weak you lend such measure of courage
As after a single gulp allays their palsy
When faced with the wrath of monarchs, or unsheathed
    weapons.
Bacchus and Venus (if she will condescend),
The arm-linked Graces in unclad sorority,
And vigil lamps will honor you all night long
Till Phoebus, with punctual bustle, banishes starlight.

HORACE III.xxi

# A Prayer to Twin Divinities

Let the girls sing of Diana in joyful praise
And the boys of her twin, Apollo unshorn, shall sing
And honor their sacred mother, whom Jupiter, king
Of gods, so favored, honor with song and the bays.

Of Diana let the girls sing, goddess of streams
Who loves the icy mountain, the darkened leafage
Of the Erymanthian woods, the brighter boscage
Of Lycian heights, young girls, give her your hymns.

To Tempe, to Phoebus Apollo's native isle
Give praise, you boys, and praise many times over
His godly shoulder slung with both lyre and quiver,
His brother's instrument, his festive, sacred soil.

Hearing your prayers, Apollo, god-begotten,
Will fend off war and plague and all ill omen
From Caesar and his people, and banish famine
To the lands of the barbarous Parthian and Briton.

HORACE I.xxi

# Miriam

I had a nice voice once, and a large following.
I was, you might say, a star.
Of course, today, no one would ever know it.
My brothers have managed to corner all the attention
In spite of some rather dubious behavior.
O I could sing and dance with the best of them,
Pattern my feet to the jubilant hosannas.
But now I am always silent, always veiled,
Not only in public but in my private chambers
Where there are no mirrors or polished surfaces
In which my white affliction could be reflected.
I've even given up going through my scrapbooks;
The past is past; it's no good to anyone.
Many were lovely once, at least as children.

# Witness

Against the enormous rocks of a rough coast
The ocean rams itself in pitched assault
And spastic rage to which there is no halt;
Foam-white brigades collapse; but the huge host

Has infinite reserves; at each attack
The impassive cliffs look down in gray disdain
At scenes of sacrifice, unrelieved pain,
Figured in froth, aquamarine and black.

Something in the blood-chemistry of life,
Unspeakable, impressive, undeterred,
Expresses itself without needing a word
In this sea-crazed Empedoclean Strife.

It is a scene of unmatched melancholy,
Weather of misery, cloud cover of distress,
To which there are no witnesses, unless
One counts the briny, tough and thorned sea holly.

# Lapidary Inscription
## with
## Explanatory Note


There was for him no more perfect epitaph
Than this from Shakespeare: "Nothing in his life
Became him like the leaving it." All those
Who knew him wished the son of a bitch in hell,
Despised his fawning sycophancy, smug
Self-satisfaction, posturing ways and pig-
Faced beady little eyes, his trite
Mind, and attested qualities of a shit,
And felt the world immeasurably improved
Right from the very moment that he left it.

———

Quintus, as what is called a man of the world,
You know how we keep the wheels of progress oiled
By what we call *prospicientia,*
*Vorsichtichkeit,* the prudent Boy Scout way
Of being prepared. For the obituary notice
When you shall slip behind the Great Portcullis,
I have prepared the modest sketch above
Conscientiously while you are still alive,
Omitting your worst features, as it behooves,
Not out of some *de mortuis* piety
But simply because they wouldn't be believed.

# Long-Distance Vision

How small they seem, those men way in the distance.
Somehow they seem scarcely to move at all,
   And when they do, it is slowly,
Almost unwillingly. I bend my head
To my writing, look up half an hour later,
   And there they are, as if

Engaged in boring discussion, fixed in a world
Almost eventless, where it is somehow always
   Three in the afternoon,
The best part of the day already wasted,
And nothing to do till it's time for the first drink
   Of the uneventful evening.

I know, of course, binoculars would reveal
They are actually doing something—one doubles over
   (Is it with pain or laughter?),
Another hangs his jacket on the handle
Of his bicycle, tucks in his Versace sport-shirt
   And furtively checks his fly.

But the naked eyesight smooths and simplifies,
And they stand as if awaiting the command
   Of a photographer
Who, having lined them up in a formal group,
Will tell them to hold even stiller than they seem
   Till he's ready to dismiss them.

In much the same way, from a palace window,
The king might have viewed a tiny, soundless crowd
      On a far hill assembled,
Failing to see what a painter would have recorded:
The little domes, immaculate in their whiteness,
      At the foot of the cross.

# Secrets

*The number of witches and sorceresses [has] everywhere become enormous.* —JOHN JEWEL, BISHOP OF SALISBURY, 1559

When they fly through the air they turn invisible
But may sometimes be spotted by patient birding questers
At the witching hour in woods on the darkest possible
Moonless nights at the regular secret musters
Of their kindred spirits, these horrible Weird Sisters.

It is widely believed that lust is their ruling passion,
A legacy maybe of Puritan tradition,
Or because they are ugly, for they use some glutinous potion
To lure young farmhands into abject submission
Or orgies of loose sabbatical possession.

For their foul rites they render the fat of babies;
Spider and warted toad mix in their simples;
Heartless they are, and death is among their hobbies;
Nothing on earth is vile as their mildest foibles,
Cold as their tits, delicate as their thimbles.

# Poppy

It builds like unseen fire deep in a mine,
    This igneous, molten wrath,
This smelting torture that rises with the decline
    Of reason, signifying death.

As when, fueled with suspicion, the coal-black
    Othello is wrought forge-hot,
Or when pouting Achilles lashes back
    At the whole Trojan lot

For the death of Patroclus: the one prepared to die
    In fury, to pit his life
Against a well-armed equal, the other to slay
    An innocent young wife;

Both, curiously, heroes. It is like that seething
    Pit, pitch-black, at whose lip
A petaled flame spreads crimsonly, bequeathing
    One or another sleep.

# The Ceremony of Innocence

He was taken from his cell, stripped, blindfolded,
And marched to a noisy room that smelled of sweat.
Someone stamped on his toes; his scream was stopped
By a lemon violently pushed between his teeth
And sealed with friction tape behind his head.
His arms were tied, the blindfold was removed
So he could see his tormentors, and they could see
The so-much-longed-for terror in his eyes.
And one of them said, "The best part of it all
Is that you won't even be able to pray."
When they were done with him, two hours later,
They learned that they had murdered the wrong man.
And this made one of them thoughtful. Some years after,
He quietly severed connections with the others,
Moved to a different city, took holy orders,
And devoted himself to serving God and the poor,
While the intended victim continued to live
On a walled estate, sentried around the clock
By a youthful, cell phone–linked praetorian guard.

# The Road to Damascus

What happened? At first there were strange, confused
    accounts.
This man, said one, who had long for righteousness' sake
Delivered unto the death both men and women
In his zeal for the Lord, had tumbled from his mount,
Felled by an unheard Word and worded omen.
Another claimed his horse shied at a snake.

Yet a third, that he was convulsed by the onslaught
Of the falling sickness, whose victims we were urged
To spit upon as protection and in disgust.
Rigid in body now as in doctrine, caught
In a seizure known but to few, he lay in the dust,
Of all his fiercest resolves stunningly purged.

We are told by certain learned doctors that those
Thus stricken are granted an inkling of that state
Where *There Shall Be No More Time*, as it is said;
As though from a pail, spilled water were to repose
Midair in pebbles of clarity, all its weight
Turned light, in a glittering, loose, but stopped cascade.

The Damascene culprits now could rest untroubled,
Their delinquencies no longer the concern
Of this fallen, converted Pharisee. He rather
From sighted blindness to blind sight went hobbled
And was led forth to a house where he would turn
His wrath from one recusancy to another.

# Elders

*Ein dunkeler Schacht ist Liebe*

As a boy he was awkward, pimpled, unpopular,
Disdained by girls, avoided by other boys,
An acned solitary. But bold and spectacular
The lubricious dreams that such a one enjoys.

He wandered apart, picked at his scabs, pinned down,
In the plush, delirious Minsky's of his mind,
High-breasted, long-thighed sirens who served his own
Terrible lusts, to which they became resigned,

And he thought himself masterful and accursed
As he pumped his flesh to climax, picturing wild
Virgins imploring him to do his worst,
And every morning he left his bedding soiled.

And so it went year by tormented year,
His yearnings snarled in some tight, muddled sensation
Of violence, a gout of imperiousness, fear
And resentment yeasting in ulcered incubation.

When he was old he encountered someone else
Enslaved by similar dreams and forbidden seethings,
Another dissatisfied, thrummed by the same pulse,
Who brought him where they both could observe bathing

In innocent calm voluptuous Susanna,
Delicate, and a quarter of his age,
Her flesh as white and wonderful as manna,
Exciting them both to desires engorged with rage.

# Sarabande on Attaining the Age
of Seventy-seven

*The harbingers are come. See, see their mark;*
*White is their colour, and behold my head.*

Long gone the smoke-and-pepper childhood smell
Of the smoldering immolation of the year,
Leaf-strewn in scattered grandeur where it fell,
Golden and poxed with frost, tarnished and sere.

And I myself have whitened in the weathers
Of heaped-up Januarys as they bequeath
The annual rings and wrongs that wring my withers,
Sober my thoughts and undermine my teeth.

The dramatis personae of our lives
Dwindle and wizen; familiar boyhood shames,
The tribulations one somehow survives,
Rise smokily from propitiatory flames

Of our forgetfulness until we find
It becomes strangely easy to forgive
Even ourselves with his clouding of the mind,
This cinerous blur and smudge in which we live.

A turn, a glide, a quarter-turn and bow,
The stately dance advances; these are airs
Bone-deep and numbing as I should know by now,
Diminishing the cast, like musical chairs.

# I.M.E.M.

To spare his brother from having to endure
Another agonizing bedside vigil
With sterile pads, syringes but no hope,
He settled all his accounts, distributed
Among a few friends his most valued books,
Weighed all in mind and heart and then performed
The final, generous, extraordinary act
Available to a solitary man,
Abandoning his translation of Boileau,
Dressing himself in a dark well-pressed suit,
Turning the lights out, lying on his bed,
Having requested neighbors to wake him early
When, as intended, they would find him dead.

# "The Darkness and the Light
Are Both Alike to Thee"

*Psalms 139:12*

Like trailing silks, the light
Hangs in the olive trees
As the pale wine of day
Drains to its very lees:
Huge presences of gray
Rise up, and then it's night.

Distantly lights go on.
Scattered like fallen sparks
Bedded in peat, they seem
Set in the plushest darks
Until a timid gleam
Of matins turns them wan,

Like the elderly and frail
Who've lasted through the night,
Cold brows and silent lips,
For whom the rising light
Entails their own eclipse,
Brightening as they fail.

# Notes

"Mirror": *A Mirror for Magistrates,* a sequence of poems by many hands concerning the theme of the Fall of Princes, of men of great authority and power, containing an *Induction,* and an account of the downfall of Henry, Duke of Buckingham, both by Thomas Sackville, Earl of Dorset.

"Samson": Judges 13:1–5

"Rara Avis in Terris": The poem was composed to accompany the anniversary gift of a brooch described in the final stanza.

"A Fall": *Pisse-Vache,* mentioned by Byron in an October 9, 1816, letter to John Murray as "one of the finest torrents in Switzerland."

"Haman": Esther 3:5–11

"A Certain Slant": The poem had its origin in a sentence in a story called "The Boys," by Anton Chekhov.

"Saul and David": I Samuel 16:14–23

"The Hanging Gardens of Tyburn": The poem is based on folklore concerning the mandrake plant, which was long believed to have magic properties. According to one botanical handbook, "its roots were an integral part of every witch's cauldron, its berries . . . used as an opiate and love potion. It was common knowledge in medieval times that the mandrake grew under the gallows from the dripping semen of hanged men. Pulled from the ground the root emitted wild shrieks and those who heard them were driven mad" (*Folklore and Symbolism of Flowers, Plants and Trees,* by Ernst and Johanna Lehner, p. 91).

"Judith": Judith 10:1–23

"Lot's Wife": Genesis 19:15–28

"Sacrifice": Genesis 22:1–19

"The Witch of Endor": I Samuel 28:3–25

"The Bequest": Vaillant, a.k.a. Pierre Chastellain (though by some these are held to be two entirely different persons) was a member of the circle of Charles d'Orléans.

"Miriam": Exodus 15:20f; Numbers 12:1–15; Deuteronomy 24:9

"Secrets": One of the folk names for the foxglove is "witch's thimbles."

"The Road to Damascus": Acts 9. See also *From Jesus to Paul*, by Joseph Klausner, pp. 325–30.

"Elders": Daniel 13; Minsky's was a striptease/burlesque theater in the Times Square area of Broadway in the late 1930s.

## A Note About the Author

Anthony Hecht is the author of seven books of poetry, among them *The Hard Hours*, which received the Pulitzer Prize for poetry in 1968, and, more recently, *Flight Among the Tombs*. In 1984 he received the Eugenio Montale Award for a lifetime achievement in poetry, and in 2000 the Robert Frost Medal from the Poetry Society of America. He has written a critical study of the poetry of W. H. Auden, and *On the Laws of the Poetic Art* (Andrew W. Mellon Lectures in the Fine Arts). He taught for some years at Bard College, the University of Rochester and Georgetown University, and now lives in Washington, D.C.

## A Note on the Type

This book was set in a typeface called Walbaum. The original cutting of the face was made by Justus Erich Walbaum (1768–1839) in Weimar in 1810. The type was revived by the Monotype Corporation in 1934. Young Walbaum began his artistic career as an apprentice to a maker of cookie molds. How he managed to leave this field and become a successful punch cutter remains a mystery. Although the type that bears his name may be classified as modern, numerous slight irregularities in its cut give this face its humane manner.

*Composed by NK Graphics, Keene, New Hampshire*

*Printed and bound by Edwards Brothers, Ann Arbor, Michigan*

*Designed by Soonyoung Kwon*